D0845570

Rumble Bus

Written by Larry Dane Brimner • Illustrated by Ronnie Rooney

The Child's World®

Published in the United States of America by The Child's World®
PO Box 326 • Chanhassen, MN 55317-0326
800-599-READ • www.childsworld.com

Reading Adviser

Cecilia Minden-Cupp, PhD, Director of Language and Literacy, Harvard University Graduate School
of Education, Cambridge, Massachusetts

Acknowledgments

The Child's World®: Mary Berendes, Publishing Director

Editorial Directions, Inc.: E. Russell Primm, Editorial Director and Project Manager; Katie Marsico,
Associate Editor; Judith Shiffer, Assistant Editor; Matt Messbarger, Editorial Assistant

The Design Lab: Kathleen Petelinsek, Design and art production

Library of Congress Cataloging-in-Publication Data

Brimner, Larry Dane.
    Rumble bus / written by Larry Dane Brimner ; illustrated by Ronnie Rooney.
        p. cm. – (Magic door to learning)
    Summary: Passengers get on and off the bus, providing a lesson in addition and subtraction.
    ISBN 1-59296-524-5 (library bound : alk. paper) [1. Addition–Fiction. 2. Subtraction–Fiction.
3. Mathematics–Fiction. 4. Buses–Fiction. 5. Stories in rhyme.] I. Rooney, Ronnie, ill. II. Title.
    PZ8.3.B77145Rum 2005
    [E]–dc22   2005005373

A book is a door, a magic door.
It can take you places
you have never been before.
Ready? Set?
Turn the page.
Open the door.
Now it is time to explore.

Rumble! Rumble!
Here comes the bus,
the Rumble Bus.

Step up. Step up.
Won't you fill the bus,
this empty Rumble Bus?
One climbs up.
The doors swing shut.

There are 11 seats left to fill today.

We had better
be on our way.

Rumble! Rumble!
Here comes the bus,
the Rumble Bus.
Step up. Step up.
Won't you fill the bus,
this yellow Rumble Bus?
Five climb up.
The doors swing shut.

There are 6 seats
left to fill today.

We don't want to be late.
Let's go on our way.

Rumble! Rumble!
Here comes the bus,
the Rumble Bus.
Step up. Step up.
Won't you fill the bus,
this squeaky Rumble Bus?
Four climb up.
The doors swing shut.

There are 2 seats left to fill today.

Oh, look at the time!
We must be on our way.

Rumble! Rumble!
Here comes the bus,
the Rumble Bus.
Step up. Step up.
Won't you fill the bus,
this noisy Rumble Bus?
Two climb up.
The doors swing shut.

Rumble! Rumble!
Here comes the bus,
a stuffed Rumble Bus,
and it's right on time.

Twelve hop off, but
the driver must stay.

Our story is over, but there is still much to explore beyond the magic door!

Do you ride the bus to school? If you do, you can practice your subtraction. How many empty seats are on the bus when you get on? As more riders hop aboard, keep track of how many of those seats fill up. How many empty seats are left by the time you reach school? Is this number the same every day?

These books will help you explore at the library and at home:

Moran, Cindy, Lisa Moran, and Joe Mathieu (illustrator). *Big Cindy's School Bus*. New York: Random House, 2004.

Roth, Carol, and Pamela Paparone (illustrator). *The Little School Bus*. New York: North-South Books, 2002.

About the Author

Larry Dane Brimner is an award-winning author of more than 120 books for children. When he isn't at his computer writing, he can be found biking in Colorado or hiking in Arizona. You can visit him online at *www.brimner.com*.

About the Illustrator

Ronnie Rooney studied painting at the University of Massachusetts Amherst and illustration at Savannah College of Art and Design. She lives in Massachusetts in a small cottage near the beach. She loves dogs and art, and would love to have a dog that could create art. So far, she has been unsuccessful in her training efforts!